HOW JOSEPH MET THE PRESIDENT

by Leola Wilkerson-Williams

Illustrated by Willie F. Vine

Balboa Press books may be ordered through booksellers or by contacting:

Balboa Press
A Division of Hay House
1663 Liberty Drive
Bloomington, IN 47403
www.balboapress.com
844-682-1282

Because of the dynamic nature of the Internet, any web addresses or links contained in this book may have changed since publication and may no longer be valid. The views expressed in this work are solely those of the author and do not necessarily reflect the views of the publisher, and the publisher hereby disclaims any responsibility for them.

Any people depicted in stock imagery provided by Getty Images are models, and such images are being used for illustrative purposes only.
Certain stock imagery © Getty Images.

ISBN: 978-1-4525-8093-7 (sc)
ISBN: 978-1-4525-8094-4 (e)

Library of Congress Control Number: 2013915391

Print information available on the last page.

Balboa Press rev. date: 01/16/2024

BALBOA.PRESS
A DIVISION OF HAY HOUSE

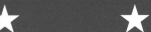

DEDICATION

This book is dedicated in memory of:
My Mother, Albertha Wilkerson
My father, Rev. David Wilkerson,
My Mother-in-law, Nancy J. Williams, and
My Father-in-law, Lawrence A. Williams, Sr.

SPECIAL THANKS

To my Heavenly Father for making this book possible;
to the White House Public Relations Staff for the
photos; to former President Bill Clinton; to LeNeisha
Paige, DaNa Perry and Byron Williams for typesetting,
and to Paula Jarriel for her encouragement.

This is Joseph Leonard Williams, when he was 9 years old. He lives in Jacksonville, Florida.

This is a picture of Joseph when he was a baby. He was born at Baptist Medical Center in Jacksonville, FL.

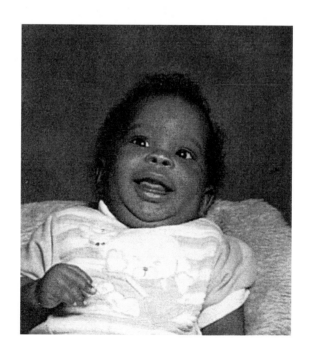

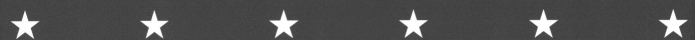

In July 1992, Joseph was dedicated to the Lord by Pastor Benny Hinn. Here is a copy of his Certificate of Dedication.

A Certificate of Dedication

This certifies that

Joseph Leonard Williams

Born 8-5-91   At Jacksonville, Fl.
        Date   Place

Was Dedicated to God

On   July 26, 1992
                Date

Place Orlando Christian Center

_____
        Minister

Leola Williams
        Mother

Lafayette H. Williams, Sr.
        Father

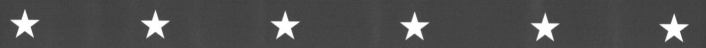

This is a photo of Joseph's parents, Leola and Lafayette Williams, Sr.

This is a picture of his brothers, Langston and Lafayette Williams, Jr. who grew up in the home with him.

Here is a photo of his oldest brother, Byron Williams, his wife, Leontyne and their children, Byron II and Lauren. They live in Fayetteville, GA.

This is a photo of Joseph's maternal grandmother, Mrs. Albertha Wilkerson. She died in 2002 in Jacksonville, Florida.

On September 19, 1995, Joseph and his mother heard on the morning news that President Clinton would be in Jacksonville that day. He was coming to walk a beat with former Sheriff, Nathaniel Glover. The newsman said "He will be speaking at Carville Park." Here are two pictures of the park.

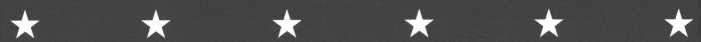

Joseph's mother told him that they were going to see the President! She decided to make a sign for the President and he helped. The sign read, "We love President Clinton." She got the idea for the sign from the NBC Today Show. Here is a sketch of that sign.

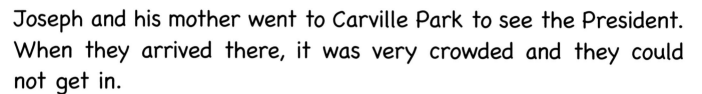

Joseph and his mother went to Carville Park to see the President. When they arrived there, it was very crowded and they could not get in.

A policeman directed them to go to the car wash off Lem Turner Road. He said "You can see the President as he will step out of his limousine to shake hands with the people along the street."

Joseph's mother drove her car near the car wash on Lem Turner Road.

They had to walk about two blocks before they saw the crowd of people waiting for the President of the United States. Everyone had to get behind some long yellow ticker tape. The secret servicemen and news people were all around.

This was a very exciting day in Joseph's life. As the President's Limousine came down the street, he got out of it. He began to walk down the street and to greet and to shake hands with the people.

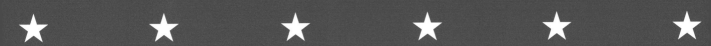

When the President noticed Joseph's sign, he told his cameraman to take their picture.

The crowd was so excited! Joseph's mother was not near him when the picture was taken. She came up a little later to meet and to shake the President's hand. She told the President that Joseph was her son. When Joseph was asked later about meeting the President he said "I met the Prince."

Here is Joseph pictured with President William "Bill" Clinton, the 42nd President of the United States of America.

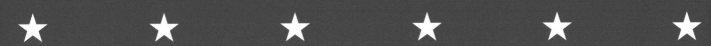

Here is another picture of Joseph with President Bill Clinton.

"...With men it is impossible, but not with God: for with God all things are possible."

St. Mark 10:27

Here is a photo of Joseph with Deborah Gianoulis, former Newswoman, of WJXT, Channel 4 in Jacksonville, FL.

...ed in the United States
...aker & Taylor Publisher Services